GIANT LIZARDS

The Ultimate Guide

Susan Creighton, M.Ed.

ONE LIFE
PUBLISHING

CHICAGO, ILLINOIS

Susan Creighton

DEDICATION

To Erin, Andy, and Chris

CONTENTS

ACKNOWLEDGMENTS

Many thanks are owed the scientists and field research assistants who spend years observing these giant lizards and documenting their habits. Often, they put their own lives in danger to do so. Also appreciation is due to the photographers whose artistry with a camera is responsible for the breathtaking photos which accompany this text. No doubt about it: a picture IS worth a thousand words. And finally, a debt of gratitude goes out to the many students, over the years, whose curiosity and thirst for knowledge prompted the production of this book.

Cover photo credit: buzzle.com

Title page photo credit: Jesse Cohen, National Zoological Park (Washington, DC)

A Komodo dragon lizard   Credit: baliassociates.com

1 INTRODUCTION: DEFINITELY GIANTS!

When we met him on the trail, he would often advance instead of running away; he'd hiss, open his mouth wide, inflate his throat, and bow his tail and body in a threatening posture." ~ Walter Auffenberg

A monster, you say? Maybe a dragon? But are there such things as dragons today? The late Dr. Walter Auffenberg of the University of Florida knew there were, and we can still find them today, on the Indonesian Archipelago. This includes the island of Komodo, after which the largest living lizard in the world is named.

Dr. Auffenberg was a **herpetologist** – a scientist who studies reptiles and amphibians. Dr. Auffenberg's interest was the study of one particular group of lizards. This group is called the monitors and includes the largest lizards in the world.

And what was the creature that Dr. Auffenberg met on the trail many years ago? Why, none other than the Komodo dragon lizard, the world's largest living monitor. The Komodo dragon can span ten feet (3 meters) from snout to tail. No wonder the doctor was careful to stay out of its way!

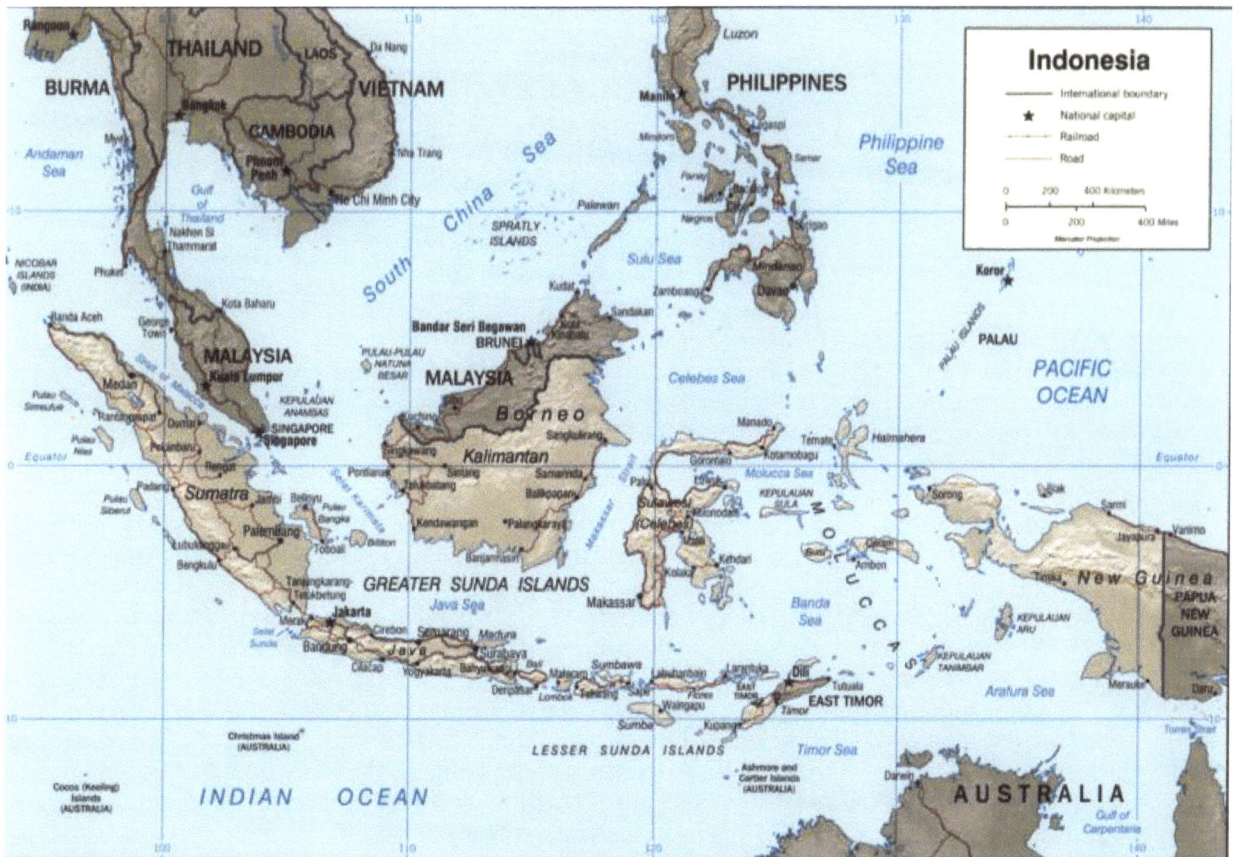

The really giant lizards come from Indonesia.   Credit: Nichalp, Central Intelligence Agency, 2003 (Wikimedia Commons)

The giant lizards living today can be traced back about 130 million years. They seem to have come from a family of now-extinct lizards called **mosasaurs**. Mosasaurs were water lizards whose bodies were well-suited to life in the sea. Their flat tails and paddle-like feet made them excellent swimmers. Their long jaws and sharp, curved teeth made catching fish an easy task. Some of the mosasaurs were more than 30 feet long (9 m)! It's a fact that the giant lizards of today had giants in their family tree.

The biggest mosasaur was Megalania. It is thought to have lived in what is now Australia more than a million years ago. The first fossil mosasaur was discovered in 1780 in Maastricht, a town in what was then the Spanish Netherlands.

The monitor lizards of today have the same ancestors as snakes. Most herpetologists agree that the forked tongue and movable lower jaw of the monitor make it a snake relative. The monitor's quick, darting tongue is used in much the same way as a snake's, to pick up particles from the air or the ground. These are then passed to the smelling organ, called the "Jacobson's organ," in the roof of the mouth. Both the lizard and the snake "smell" with this organ.

There are about 31 types of monitor lizards known today. Of these, about 16 will reach the length of three feet (0.9 m) or more as adults. Compared to the average lizard which measures only 4 to 12 inches (10 to 30 centimeters), the large monitors really are "giant lizards" in the reptile family.

Credit: komodonationalpark.org

Komodo National Park is home to many species of animal, including the Komodo dragon lizard. The Park is located approximately in the center of the Archipelago, between the islands of Sumbawa and Flores. Here, the biodiversity of the area – both land and sea – is protected. The Park covers three large islands – Komodo, Rinca, and Padar – as well as several smaller islands. It provides a refuge for more than 1,000 species of fish, hundreds of reef-building coral species, and numerous sponges, dugong, sharks, and manta rays. In addition, many whales, dolphins and sea turtles can also be found at the Park. Komodo National Park is an important biosphere protecting the many animal and plant species who make it their home.

Dr. Walter Auffenberg (February 26, 1928 – January 17, 2004), the renowned American herpetologist, spent almost forty years in the field studying reptile and amphibian paleontology, as well as the biology and habits of alligators and Komodo dragons. In 1969, Dr. Auffenberg and his family moved to Komodo Island so that he could study the Komodo dragon in its natural habitat. He and his research assistant captured and tagged more than fifty Komodo dragons which they studied, and Dr. Auffenberg later wrote *The Behavioral Ecology of the Komodo Monitor*, the book for which he is most famous. His life work directed the world's attention to this amazing animal and stimulated the protection and propagation of Komodo dragons in captivity. Today, the Denver Zoo is quite proactive in breeding these reptiles.

Varanus komodoensis

The Komodo dragon lizard *(Varanus komodoensis)* is a giant lizard found among several islands of the Indonesian Archipelago. The species belongs to the monitor lizard family (Varanidae). Their large size can be attributed to the fact that there were and are no other carnivorous animals in their habitat that could prey upon them. Fossils similar to *V. komodoensis* have been found in Australia, suggesting that the species may have lived throughout Indonesia and Australia but some populations perhaps died out as their preferred fauna prey disappeared, or perhaps as the arrival of hominids caused their numbers to dwindle. Today, the Komodo dragon is **endemic** to a few small islands in the Archipelago. Aside from zoos, the species can only be found on these few islands. There may be only 5,000 Komodo dragons currently living in the wild.

Kingdom: Animalia
Phylum: Chordata
Class: Reptilia
Order: Squamata
Suborder: Lacertilia
Family: Varanaidae
Genus: *Varanus*
Subgenus: *V. (Varanus)*
Species: *V. komodoensis*

A Komodo dragon lizard .   Credit: Dezidor (Wikimedia Commons)

A Komodo dragon lizard.

Credit: Midori (Wikimedia Commons)

2 PORTRAIT OF THE GIANTS

Monitor lizards live in the warmer parts of Africa, Asia, the East Indies, and Australia. No monitors are native to North or South America.

Heat is especially important to monitors because they are **ectothermic** (cold blooded animals whose bodies take on the same temperature as their surroundings). At night and on cool mornings, their body temperatures are low, and the monitors are relatively inactive. To hunt actively for prey, they must first absorb enough heat from the sun to warm their bodies to their ideal temperatures, which vary from species to species. For this reason, monitor lizards are **diurnal**. This means they are busy during the day and sleep or rest at night. (This is in contrast to some animals which are **nocturnal**, or active at night while sleeping during the day.) In cold seasons, monitors become inactive, much like a bear that hibernates through the winter.

Keen senses and special features

All monitors have excellent vision and a very keen sense of smell. The Komodo dragon is no exception. Since their eyes are positioned on either side of the head, monitors do not have **binocular vision** like humans. They take cues from each eye separately, which is called **monocular vision**. This feature gives them an increased field of view, but their depth perception is limited. Their eyesight is very good for detecting quick movements or food at a distance. Monitors usually locate food visually before chasing it. But they can smell dead or decaying prey several miles away.

A monitor's legs are ideal for climbing, swimming, or running. Each of the monitor's four powerful legs ends in five clawed toes. The claws are long and curved, perfect for pinning down prey or fighting.

The claws are also useful in grasping the bark of a tree and pulling the lizard up and away from danger. A monitor's grasp is extremely strong. Herpetologists Sherman and Madge Minton told of a story they heard many years ago:

"Several times while we were in Asia we heard stories of monitors being used as living grappling hooks by burglars or soldiers attacking walled villages. The lizard, with a rope tied around its body just in front of the hind legs, climbs up a wall. When it reaches the top, the burglar or soldier holding the rope gives a tug, the lizard digs in its claws and holds on, and the man pulls himself up the rope!"

Although the Mintons could not confirm the story and suspected it might be a local folk tale, they admitted that there was nothing impossible about the story. The monitors' strength is well-documented.

Monitors have tapered heads with ear openings at either side, long and slender necks, and movable eyelids. Their nasal openings may be at the front tip of the head or nearer to their eyes. (Komodo dragons' nasal openings are near the front tip of their heads.) Monitors, of course, have lungs, not gills, so they must breathe air to fill their lungs. But the more aquatic monitors are able to remain submerged for fairly long periods of time. Scientists believe that they may be able to seal off their nasal openings to prevent water from entering. Monitors frequently escape from a fight or from human predators by diving into the water and swimming away underwater. One species, the Nile monitor, can remain underwater for as long as one hour!

As for hearing, monitors must rely more on sight and smell. Although they do have visible earholes on either side of their heads, their sense of hearing is not very acute.

A Komodo dragon's mouth and teeth.

Jaws and teeth

The jaws of a monitor are powerful, and when the lizard clamps down on something it hangs on fiercely. Both upper and lower jaws are movable. The lower jaw can be extended by means of the lizard's **hyoid apparatus** (expandable joints at the rear of the lower jaw). This gives the monitor a larger mouth cavity and lets it swallow its prey whole, like a snake does.

The teeth are arranged in two rows, one on each of the movable jaws. A monitor's teeth are somewhat flat, curved back, and serrated like a knife. The monitor's teeth, combined with its sharp claws, make it a formidable predator. An animal lucky enough to escape from the jaws of a monitor may still die from the wounds inflicted by those sharp teeth.

Gray's monitor is the one exception to the rule. While all monitors are carnivores and eat meat, Gray's monitor has a diet high in fruit and tree snails. Its rounded peg-like teeth are better suited to its special diet.

Even though they have powerful jaws and teeth, monitors do not make many sounds. Most of the sounds they produce are not vocalizations. For instance, when monitors eat, they frequently sneeze to remove fly larvae from their nasal passages. A male may scratch his claws on the female's scales during courtship, producing a scratching noise. Perhaps the only significant sound a monitor makes is its fearsome hissing, which is common in displays of aggression.

Monitor lizard using its tongue as a scent organ.   Credit: pbase.com

Mouth

The mouth of a monitor lizard is a dangerous place for both animals and humans. Besides their powerful jaws and teeth, most of the larger monitors produce a bacteria-laced saliva which can cause the death of a prey animal who manages to escape. If the monitor's teeth break the skin of a human or animal, the saliva sets up an infection in the victim's bloodstream which, if not treated immediately, usually leads to death. Monitors have been known to follow prey which have escaped as if they "knew" that eventually the animal would become severely ill and the lizard could capture it once again, this time for good.

In addition to the seriously dangerous bacteria which is found in most monitors' mouths, scientists believe they have discovered venom-producing glands in some species. In 2005, researchers at the University of Melbourne found that the Perentie produces a venom which helps to weaken and immobilize its prey. The Lace monitor, the Spotted Tree monitor, and of course the Komodo dragon are also believed to produce a venom or venom-like substance. It is not yet clear whether all monitor lizards produce such a poison, but it does seem likely.

When a human is bitten by a monitor lizard, swelling, poor bloodclotting, and shooting pains ensue. These symptoms may be due to the venom the lizard injects into the victim. In 2001, Phil Bronstein, an executive of the San Francisco Chronicle newspaper, was invited by an animal keeper into the enclosure of a Komodo dragon lizard at the Los Angeles zoo. Monitor lizards in captivity often appear to be docile and mild-mannered. The keeper asked Bronstein to take off his white shoes, as they might resemble the white rats that the Komodo was fed and might excite the animal. Even though he removed his shoes, Bronstein was bitten on his bare foot by the Komodo dragon, severing a tendon and seriously infecting his foot. After months of treatment and rehabilitation, Bronstein recovered. On other occasions, children who had been allowed to pet the dragon lizard had also been taken to the hospital suffering from salmonella infections. Like most reptiles, monitor lizards can carry the salmonella bacteria on their skin.

Monitor lizard swallowing a fish whole .   Credit: gundamseed84, www.clubsnap.com/forums/world-nature

The monitor's tongue, as has been stated before, is used primarily as an organ of smell. Unlike other lizards, monitors do not appear to have taste buds. The voracious manner in which they eat their prey – whole, without apparently tasting it – gives credibility to the theory that taste buds, if present, are not very important to the monitor's mealtime procedures.

Tasting is known as **gustation.** In animals who eat their prey whole, like alligators and monitor lizards, gustation may not be as important as it is in animals who "sample" their food before swallowing it. Snakes and lizards with forked tongues use their Jacobson's organs to smell-taste their food; real taste buds may not be necessary to such species.

Scales

The body of a monitor is covered with small scales that do not overlap. Scales help reduce water loss and let the monitor absorb heat from the sun. The scaly skin is thick and tough and acts like a suit of armor. Monitors have small, grainy scales over most of their bodies. Spiny scales appear in selected places for added protection, such as around the anal opening and on the head and neck.

New scales are formed by the tissues underlying the lizard's existing scales. When the new scales are fully formed, lizards shed their old skin. (This is another similarity between monitor lizards and snakes.)

Young monitors have more brightly colored scales which grow duller as the animals grow older. The bright colors may help to conceal the young that spend most of their time in the tree limbs of their habitats.

Adult monitors vary in color. Komodo dragons are grey-brown with red circles over their entire body. The two-banded water monitor is brown to black with yellowish bands above, and white or cream-colored below. The Australian Perentie has an ivory-colored neck with a coarse black network pattern over the rest of its body. The markings of the Nile monitor consist of yellow bands and spots on a greenish background. The Lace monitor is typically blue-black above with scattered white or yellow on the body, tail, and limbs.

A Komodo dragon shows off its mouth cavity.   Credit: Mike Gadell, http://mikegadell.files.wordpress.com

Useful tails

In general, the tail of a monitor is thick and long (often more than half the total body length). The short-tailed monitor is the exception.

A few smaller monitors have **prehensile tails**. These tails grasp tree branches and wrap around them, enabling the monitors to move from tree to tree. The giant lizards, however, do not have prehensile tails. They spend their time on the ground or in the water, where their tails are used primarily for balance, defense, and as a rudder in swimming. They can also injure small prey with one swipe of their tail.

Scientists have noted that a monitor does not have the ability to regrow its tail as the smaller lizards do. (This property is called **regeneration**.) A fight, therefore, sometimes results in a monitor losing part of its tail. The lost part does not grow back.

Along with its natural defenses, a monitor lizard often uses **posturing** to frighten off its predators, just as some other animals do. Posturing involves sticking their heads high in the air, puffing out their throats, expanding their ribcage, and whipping their tails from side to side. This frightening display is often enough to send a predator running. Many animals besides monitors also use posturing to appear larger and more dangerous than they really are.

By the way, humans are known to use posturing as well. When a human accentuates his height, or the size of his shoulders, or walks in a menacing way, he is doing what animals know all too well: posturing.

A Komodo dragon's tail   Credit: simple.wikipedia.org

This Komodo dragon has lost part of its tail.   Credit: source unknown

★from the news★

This is probably *not* a good idea!   Credit: freerepublic.com

Scientists Reveal Venomous Bite of Komodo Dragon
redorbit.com/news/science ^ | 19 May 2009

by Joe ProBono

Australian researchers have discovered what makes the Komodo dragon's bite so deadly for its prey.

Scientists previously considered that the world's largest lizard's mouth held deadly bacteria that stopped its victims' blood from clotting. Walter Auffenberg put that theory forward in 1981.

But lead researcher Bryan Fry used magnetic resonance imagery to show that the deadly lizard packs a venomous bite, as seen through its venom gland with ducts that lead to their teeth.

Fry used 3-D computer imaging to compare the Komodo's bite with the bite of the Australian saltwater crocodile, which has a skull of comparable size. His team found that the Komodo's bite is only one-sixth as powerful as that of the crocodile.

Imaging revealed that the Komodo used a pulling maneuver similar to the motion of the bite of a shark or saber cat.

The report, published in the *Proceedings of the National Academy of Sciences*, also found that other venomous lizards, including the Gila monster, were part of the same family as Komodo dragons. Additionally, venomous lizards and snakes appear to have descended from common origins.

A small alligator lizard using its prehensile tail.   Credit: H. Iaoticus, scorpionforum.darkbb.com

Size and life expectancy

Monitors vary in size and weight. The smallest is the short-tailed monitor, which measures only eight inches (20 cm) long and weighs just a few ounces. The giant lizards are those that grow to at least three feet (0.9 m) long.

The real "stars" of the monitor family are: the Komodo dragon, which can reach ten feet (3 m) long and weigh up to 350 pounds (158 kilograms); the New Guinea crocodile monitor, which can be over eight feet long (2.44 m); the Asian water monitor, occasionally growing to eight or nine feet (2.4 to 2.7 m) or more in length; the Perentie, about seven feet (2.1 m) long; and the Lace monitor and Nile monitor, both measuring about six feet (1.8 m) in length.

Although the Komodo dragon is decidedly the largest monitor, it is difficult to rank monitors by size, since within each species the largest size achieved depends greatly on availability of food, life expectancy, and environmental conditions. Many native human populations hunt monitors for food, thereby shortening their lives and preventing them from reaching their greatest size. Injuries received in the wild can also make a difference in how long a monitor lives.

Some individual monitors that have been studied by herpetologists have lived fifteen years or more. However, some scientists believe that under ideal conditions monitors might live 100 years. Monitors are being kept and bred in zoos, so we may eventually know more about how long they might be able to live.

Scientific names

The giant lizards, like all animals, are identified scientifically by genus and species, Latin names which pinpoint the exact animal one is referring to. The **genus** for all monitor lizards is *Varanus,* and this is often abbreviated *V.* After the genus, the **species** name follows. The species may have been named after the scientist who first discovered or studied the species, or it may have another interesting origin.

Komodo dragon: *V. komodoensis*   Australian Perentie: *V. giganteus*
New Guinea crocodile monitor: *V. salvadorii*   African Nile monitor: *V. niloticus*
Asian water monitor: *V. salvator*   Australian Lace monitor: *V. varius*

Large monitors do not make easy house pets. Keep them in the wild!   Credit: boards.straightdope.com

★ interview ★

ROM WHITAKER, REPTILE EXPERT

Romulus ("Rom") Whitaker is the reptile expert and conservationist who travels around the world for the PBS Nature documentary program *The Dragon Chronicles.* He first became interested in reptiles as a child. Over the years he has set up a snake refuge in India, co-founded the Madras Crocodile Bank, and established India's first rainforest research station in Agumbe. Besides being a widely published author, Rom has also made many wildlife-related films. In *The Dragon Chronicles*, Rom had an opportunity to "meet" some Komodo dragon lizards. He answered a few questions for the Nature interviewer:

Were you surprised when the Komodo dragon started chasing you?

I really had no idea that Komodos would actually chase a human, but then again, why not; we must be as tasty as a deer. This was truly a surprise, and I'm glad the local guides insisted that we carry a forked stick with us and that we shouldn't walk around alone on the island.

Did you have a favorite or unexpected moment while shooting *The Dragon Chronicles*?

I think the most unexpected moment was being chased by the Komodo dragon. The other startling revelation was the dragon's immense power and stamina. I'm used to crocodiles: they're very powerful but they run out of steam very quickly when you are capturing and handling them. The dragon we caught for our saliva tests just didn't tire and his recovery time after we released him was just seconds!

What can humans learn from the "dragons" featured in the film?

Years ago it was pretty hard to get people to empathize even a little bit with scaly, cold-blooded critters; now, thanks a lot to good PR from television, it is easier to get the message of reptile conservation and tolerance across. We have a lot to be thankful to reptiles for, not the least of which is their control of rodents.

But besides their utility on the planet, our remaining dragons are needed to excite our senses, to fill every generation with renewed wonder, and to keep us alert for that predator lurking just around the corner!

See the rest of the interview at http://www.pbs.org/wnet/nature/episodes/the-dragon-chronicles/interview-rom-whitaker-reptile-expert/4525/

Photo Credit: pbs.org

★ biography ★

Photo credit: en.domotica.net

WALTER AUFFENBERG, AMERICAN HERPETOLOGIST
FEBRUARY 26, 1928 – JANUARY 17, 2004

Walter Auffenberg was an American herpetologist who also studied reptile and amphibian paleontology. His field research on the Komodo dragon lizard drew the attention of both academics and the public to this remarkable and fascinating animal, living on a few small islands in Indonesia.

He earned his Bachelor of Science in Zoology from Stetson University in Deland, Florida. He wrote his masters thesis on the morphology of the blacksnake while at the University of Florida in Gainesville, and his doctoral dissertation on fossil snakes of Florida was also completed at Gainesville.

In 1969, Dr. Auffenberg moved his wife and children to Komodo Island with him for almost a year, so that he could further research the Komodo dragon lizard in its natural habitat. His research led to a number of zoos and wildlife facilities undertaking the propagation of this species of lizard in captivity.

His most famous publication, *The Behavioral Ecology of the Komodo Monitor (1981),* is the basis of much of our knowledge of the Komodo dragon. Dr. Auffenberg also authored books on Gray's monitor and the Bengal monitor, as well as many other books on reptiles and amphibians. The Peacock monitor *(Varanus auffenbergi)* was named for him.

Dr. Auffenberg loved field research, and, during his time on the islands, he became well acquainted with more than fifty Komodo dragons. If anyone could say they knew the dragons well, he certainly could have!

Dr. Auffenberg's friends.   Credit :redorbit.com

The Giant Komodo Dragon Lizard   Credit: Oak Park (IL) Journal

3 FEEDING HABITS

In 1982, Australian engineer Keith Stewart made an unusual friend. While on a camping trip to Umbrawarra in the Australian **outback** (vast, remote, arid areas of Australia), Stewart met a "**goanna**," the Australian term for monitor lizard. This goanna was over four feet (1.2 m) long and lived in the deep green pools of a gorge where Stewart had set up camp.

Stewart playfully named the goanna Cedric. Cedric was probably a Spencer's monitor *(V. spenceri),* with brown coloring on its scales and a yellow neck. A Spencer's monitor can be any color from pale dirty cream to darker rusty brown, with scattered brown and cream spots. There may be irregular light yellow or grey cross bands on the neck, body, and tail. This monitor grows to a length of about four feet (1.2 m), not a giant by any means, but a member of the same genus as the larger lizards. As such, many of the habits of the Spencer's monitor will also be found among other species of monitor lizards.

The nostrils of a Spencer's monitor are positioned near the tip of the snout and off to each side. The tail is more or less round at its base (where it joins the body), but at its end it is compressed to resemble the keel of a boat. And, in fact, this monitor is an excellent swimmer.

Swallowing prey whole

Stewart was amazed at the monitor's great appetite and its eating habits. Here is an entry from Stewart's journal:

Cedric came out again today. I caught three fish for him, two of which he devoured in front of me. The third, being considerably larger, put up such a fight that Cedric needed all his strength just to keep its head in his mouth. He persevered, however, throwing his whole body into the struggle, arching his neck stiffly and pressing the tail of the fish hard against the ground.

His elastic reptile jaws opened wide, and he swallowed the entire fish! It took three or four minutes for him to force it down, during which time his body underwent amazing contortions. His neck must have swelled to twice its normal size as the head of the fish passed through. When the last of the tail was gone, Cedric opened his mouth wide, seeming to yawn for a moment, then turned back into the water and swam away.

Lizard using a tree to brace a fish.   Credit: citybirds.com

Nile monitor swallowing a mouse whole.   Credit: reptileforums.co.uk

Perentie lizard, also known as the "goanna."   Credit:: Steven David Miller, naturepl.com

Dragons scavenging an abandoned carcass.   Credit: myths-made-real.blogspot.com

Monitors, like snakes, swallow their prey whole when they can. If the prey is too large to swallow whole, the monitor's sharp teeth can usually crush the bones of its victim, and the monitor's powerful forelegs and claws make short work of breaking up the prey into manageable pieces.

Saliva begins to break down the monitor's food as soon as it enters the mouth cavity. A monitor's mouth has a strong, bony roof that protects the mouth from damage while eating those large mouthfuls. The elongated S-shaped necks of monitors can swell to make room for very large prey, as can their abdomens. Often, after feeding, a monitor's belly will hang down to the ground.

Waiting for prey

Monitors sometimes hunt by what is colorfully known as the "lurk 'n' lurch" method. A monitor will hide in brush and wait for its prey to come within attack distance. For a Komodo dragon, this distance is between three and four feet (0.9 and 1.2 m).

The monitor then lunges forward suddenly and grabs whatever part of the animal's body it can. It clamps down with its sharp, serrated teeth and hangs on while the animal twists and turns, trying to free itself. This struggle itself often leads to the death of the prey. The monitor's teeth may cut through blood vessels and bones, crippling the captured animal.

Monitors have been known to catch and kill animals even larger than themselves. This means the monitor may be dragged a short distance before its prey gives up. But the monitor never lets go.

Even animals that manage, somehow, to escape from the monitor's grasp are generally doomed, however. The bacteria in the monitor's mouth will eventually cause blood poisoning in the animal that has been bitten. The escaping prey may bleed to death or die from a bacterial infection.

In 2009, on the island of Komodo, two dragons mauled a human male to death. The fruit picker had fallen out of a sugar apple tree, and within minutes the dragons had bitten him numerous times on the hands, body, neck and legs. Although he was rushed to a clinic on the nearby island of Flores, he later died from his wounds. A neighbor said she saw the two dragons waiting for the man under the tree.

Although attacks on humans are rare, they are said to be increasing as the dragons' habitat becomes restricted.

Crocodile eggs: a monitor feast.   Credit: nigeldennis.com

Some unpleasant habits

Since they are **carnivores**, monitors will eat any animal that lives in their habitat. Most of these lizards are also very fond of eggs and will steal then from birds' nests, other lizards, and even a farmer's henhouse if they can get away with it. The Nile monitor is known to steal crocodile eggs, although these are usually closely guarded by the mother.

Africa.   Credit: Hoshie (Wikimedia Commons)

Monitor stealing crocodile eggs   Credit: photos.travelblog.org

The monitor is very much aware of other animals' behavior patterns. It will wait for hours for the moment when the adult animal leaves its eggs in search of food. Even humans leave a henhouse unattended sooner or later, and that's when the monitor will seize its opportunity. Many researchers have reported that their tents were all but destroyed by hungry monitors tearing through baskets and backpacks in search of food.

The large monitors also feed on crustaceans, fish, frogs, snakes, rats and birds. Monitors often eat the remains of another animal's kill (**carrion**). They can detect carrion by smell, even over long distances.

Watching giant lizards eat is not always a pretty sight. Dr. Auffenberg had many chances to observe Komodo dragons eating both live prey and carrion. He wrote:

I have observed one lizard gulp down the entire head of a wild boar; and in another instance we watched Number 28, a female weighing 110 pounds, devour 90 pounds of hog in seventeen minutes!

Dr. Wilbert Neugebauer of the Wilhelmina Zoo in Germany observed that, after eating, a monitor will lick its snout with its tongue, rub the sides of its head against the ground, and raise its head and look about. This appears to be an example of **ritual behavior** (behavior that is done automatically at specific times). It may signal to smaller lizards that they may now approach the remains of the kill and eat without fear of attack.

Smaller monitors and young monitors often instinctively roll around in the hair, intestines, and feces of carrion. Herpetologists believe this behavior protects them from being eaten by the larger monitors. Since monitors do not eat the intestines, hair, or feces of their prey, these odors on the smaller monitors keep the larger lizards away and thereby protect the smaller ones from attack.

In their role as **scavengers**, monitors help to clean up the environment by eating dead and decaying animal matter. They can make a meal out of "leftovers" that another predator leaves behind. This means that the monitor does not need to kill as often as an animal that does not eat carrion.

Dr. Auffenberg pointed out that monitors only kill when hungry. Because they need to conserve body heat by conserving energy, monitors are less likely to kill more prey than they can eat. And monitors save what they don't finish and eat it at the next meal.

Komodo dragons finishing off the remains of some prey.   Credit: members.fortunecity.com

Cannibalism

Reptiles are a lower (more primitive) form of life than mammals. They do not have a family life like wolves or elephants do. Furthermore, young lizards are not born helpless or dependent like wolf cubs or elephant calves are. Monitor lizards are able to live independently from the time they are hatched. So with no "family ties" to bind them (the lizard mother doesn't even know her own young since she leaves her eggs after depositing them), adults and hatchlings become competitors for the same food supply.

Although **cannibalism**, or the eating of their own kind, by adult monitors may seem cruel, the young are quite fast and equipped with many survival instincts of their own, such as keeping to the tree branches during non-feeding times. Only the weak or sick lizards are likely to be killed and eaten by the adults. In this way, these defective lizards are prevented from mating, and the species as a whole is strengthened.

★ biography ★

Credit: http://web.utk.edu/~gburghar/

GORDON BURGHARDT, ANIMAL PSYCHOLOGIST

Animal psychologists study the cognitive (thinking and learning) behavior of various species. Gordon Burghardt had the unique experience of working with Kraken, a Komodo dragon bred in captivity at the National Zoo in Washington, D.C. By observing the lizard's behavior in many different situations, Dr. Burghardt was able to hypothesize that large lizards have much more cognitive ability (intelligence) than previously assumed. Particularly in the area of play, Kraken showed a side of the Komodo dragon's personality that had not been studied before.

Other lizards, and other reptiles such as snakes, alligators and turtles, may have much more intelligence than they have been credited with in the past. Dr. Burghardt continues to study reptiles to help determine exactly what kind of "brain power" they have. And the results have been startling. Reptiles, which are considered to be more primitive than mammals, are certainly capable of play.

We all know that play is an important part of the development of mammals, including humans. Dr. Burghardt's book, *The Genesis of Animal Play*, is considered a breakthrough in understanding the role of play in various other classes of animals. He presents evidence of playfulness in animals we might not expect: kangaroos, birds, fish, and of course lizards.

Dr. Burghardt received his Ph.D. at the University of Chicago and is currently Alumni Distinguished Professor in Psychology and in Ecology and Evolutionary Biology at the University of Tennessee in Knoxville.

Lace monitor climbing a tree.   Credit: S. Gavins (Wikimedia Commons)

Australia.   Credit: Mark (Wikimedia Commons)

4 HOMES AND HABITATS

The large monitor lizards live in various parts of the "Old World" – parts of Asia, Africa, and Australia. Being **cold-blooded,** they depend on a warm environment and the sun to raise their body temperatures after a cool night. Without such heat, monitors could not perform the basic activities of life. All monitors spend a good part of their day basking in the sun to absorb its heat.

Because of their sharp claws, small lizards and young monitors can climb trees and stay in the lower branches for a good part of the day. When they grow to adulthood, the monitors will take their places in the water, the desert, the plains, or the jungle. Each species of monitor has a very specific **habitat** or home.

The Komodo dragon makes its home on the island of Komodo, the tiny islands of Rintja and Padar, and a small part of western Flores in the Sunda Islands of Indonesia. Dragons sleep and take shelter under thick vegetation or in burrows they dig themselves.

The two-banded water monitor ranges from Ceylon and the southern part of India to China, the Philippines, and many Indonesian islands. It, too, finds shelter under vegetation and in crevices near the water. The water monitor is probably the most aquatic of monitor lizards. It spends much of its time in the water and is an excellent swimmer.

Two-banded water monitor   Credit: bbc.co.uk   Nile monitor   Credit: reptilesalive.com

Another fine swimmer is the Nile monitor, found in Africa south of the Sahara Desert and as far south as the Cape of Good Hope. Although it prefers to live near the water, the Nile monitor can be found in nearly all parts of Africa except the desert.

Of the thirty-one species of monitors currently known, sixteen can be found in Australia. The largest of these are the Perentie and the Lace monitors. The Perentie lives in desert areas where it prefers to hide in rock crevices. The Lace monitor is a tree lizard, so it is found in those habitats where the Perentie does not live: green, brush- and tree-covered territory. The Lace monitor, though large, is quite slender, so it can move from tree to tree with ease, unlike most adult monitors.

Perentie monitor in the wild.   Credit: Kaiwhakahaere, en.wikipedia.org

★ folklore ★

The Pitjantjatjara people of Central Australia tell a story about how the Perentie and the Goanna* got their colors. Here is their story, as retold by Trephina Sultan:

How the Perentie and Goanna* Got Their Colors

The perentie (Nintaka) and the goanna (Milbili), agreed to decorate each other for a ceremony. The perentie was a good artist, who took great care with his work. So he painted the goanna with great care and skill, painting fine lines and dots over the goanna's body. When the paint had dried, he turned the goanna over and using the thinnest of brushes and the greatest of care, painted extremely fine lines on his belly.

Now it was the goanna's turn to paint the perentie. The goanna however was lazy, and because it took so long for the perentie to paint the goanna, and the time for the ceremony was drawing near, the goanna quickly painted the perentie with crude splashes of yellow dots, which he applied with pieces of rolled-up bark.

When the goanna had finished, the perentie asked how he looked. The goanna lied and said he looked beautiful. However, on the way to the ceremony, the perentie walked past a waterhole and saw his reflection in the water. The perentie was angry with how he looked, and rushed to attack the goanna, but the goanna escaped by climbing to the top of the gum tree.

The perentie cursed the goanna and said that from now on he must live in the branches of trees and take shelter in the tree hollows, while he himself would use the rocks as his home and shelter.

Today, you can see the two keep to their own habitats, still wearing the designs on their bodies: the goanna with a delicate lace-like pattern on its back, while the perentie's dark brown skin is covered with large yellow dots and irregular lines.

* * *

The story can be found published in *Australian Dreaming: 40,000 Years of Aboriginal History*, by Jennifer Isaacs, New Holland Publishing Australia Pty Ltd, 2006.

Credit: http://www.ausemade.com.au/aboriginal/resources/dreamtime/perentie-goanna.htm

*Although the term *goanna* can refer to several types of monitor lizards, in this story it is the Lace monitor that is a main character.

Merten's water monitors mating .   Credit: geckodan2003, flickr.com

Lace monitors mating.   Credit: Leanne Ronalds, flickr.com

Komodo dragon hatching from egg.   Credit: news.bbc.co.uk

5 COURTSHIP, MATING, AND YOUNG

Herpetologists have had difficulty observing the mating habits of monitors. They do not seem to have an elaborate **courtship ritual** as in some other animal species. Dr. Auffenberg noted that Komodo dragons will not mate with unfamiliar lizards just "passing through" their territory. But monitors do not develop lifelong attachments to a single mate, as geese, for example, do.

The male monitor signals his intention to mate by pursuing the female while making zigzag movements with his head. The male then grasps the female by the skin of the head or neck, pushes his tail under hers, and twists his body to bring their **cloacae** (reproductive cavities) together. The male deposits the sperm that will fertilize the female's eggs in her cloaca.

Mating usually occurs in the spring and summer. Monitors are egg-layers, so the female will deposit her eggs in a burrow or tree hollow. Hatching time varies among the different species, with the largest monitors laying the largest eggs and requiring the longest hatching time (approximately eight months for Komodo dragons).

Most monitor eggs are soft and leathery, not hard-shelled. The hatchlings bite through the egg with an "egg tooth" that protrudes from their snouts. The egg tooth is a real tooth that falls out soon after hatching.

One observation that interests herpetologists is that Nile monitors and Lace monitors lay their eggs in termite mounds! By coincidence, the temperature and humidity in a termite mound are ideal for **incubating** (warming) the eggs. For some reason which scientists do not yet understand, the termites do not disturb the lizard eggs. As soon as they hatch, the young lizards scurry out of the mound.

The largest monitors lay the fewest eggs at one time, sometimes as few as seven eggs in a **clutch**. Smaller monitors may deposit as many as thirty-four eggs at one time. When **hatchlings** finally emerge from their eggs, they have no mother to care for them, since monitors do not rear their young. The young monitors will take to the trees for the first year of life. Otherwise, they may find themselves on the menu for any adult monitors in the vicinity. Yes, adult monitors will eat their own young! The young who flee to the tree limbs will survive on insects, small birds, and eggs until they are fully grown and able to defend themselves against mature adults. This can take five years for a Komodo dragon.

Except for mating and feeding, these young monitors will live solitary lives. They will not form family groups, although they will become familiar with "who's who" in their own and surrounding territories.

★from the news★

The hatching of Kraken, 1992   Credit: Jesse Cohen, Smithsonian Institution

Difficulties of Raising Animal Populations in Captivity

The female Komodo dragon Kraken was one of over a dozen Komodo dragons hatched at the National Zoo of the Smithsonian Institute in 1992. This was the first group of this endangered species born outside Indonesia. Kraken would make headlines again twelve years later in 2004 when she died at the Zoo when an egg follicle and a blood vessel ruptured in an ovary. Kraken had reportedly suffered from reproductive tract infections before, and her death led to charges that Zoo curators and veterinarians had not done enough to prevent her death. In fact, reproductive tract infections have caused the deaths of eighteen captive Komodo dragons worldwide. *(Reported by Karla Barker of the Washington Post, 6/29/2005)*

Kraken's death is just one example of how difficult it is to raise wild animals in a controlled environment such as a zoo. Although it can be argued that Kraken might have died from similar causes had she lived in the wild, some animal advocates insist that if a zoo or other facility is not prepared to take every step necessary to insure an animal's health and comfort, then it should not be keeping animals at all.

Komodo dragon lizards are currently listed as an endangered species, and the Zoo is propagating them.

Kraken, as an adult.   Credit: Tim Knight, scienceblogs.com

Komodo dragons mating side by side at Zoo Praha.   Credit: Petr Velensky, zoopraha.cz

Parthenogenesis

Most lizards reproduce sexually. That is, there must be a male to fertilize and a female to produce eggs in which the offspring incubate. However, scientists have been discovering an ability for female lizards to reproduce even when males are not available in their environment. This asexual form of reproduction is called **parthenogenesis**. Often in these cases, mating behaviors are still seen even though there are no males present. A female lizard will play the role usually played by the male and will mount another female who is about to lay eggs, Lizards who act out this courtship ritual have great reproductive ability than females who are in isolation. Perhaps the ritual stimulates hormones needed for reproduction.

The Komodo dragon normally reproduces sexually (with both male and female present) but has been found able to reproduce asexually by parthenogenesis. The females may switch back and forth between sexual reproduction and parthenogenesis as conditions dictate. This may be one reason why Komodo dragons have been able to keep their population at between 4,000 and 5,000 individuals. When males are present, sexual reproduction occurs. When there are no males in a territory, parthenogenesis may operate.

When females reproduce by parthenogenesis, however, only male offspring are produced. No viable female lizards result. This fact may explain why the ratio of male to female Komodo dragons is about three to one. Scientists also caution that a diverse gene pool makes for healthier offspring. When a female reproduces by parthenogenesis, she is drawing only from her own genes, since she has no partner to contribute his. In the long run, parthenogenesis is not an ideal route to reproduction. But in the short run, it may permit a species, like the Komodo dragon, to continue to reproduce until more ideal conditions are present.

Lace monitor hatching from its egg.   Credit: crocdoc, captivebredreptileforums.co.uk

Some Facts About the Lizard Egg

The amniote egg, the type that lizards lay, must be fertilized internally but may be laid on land.

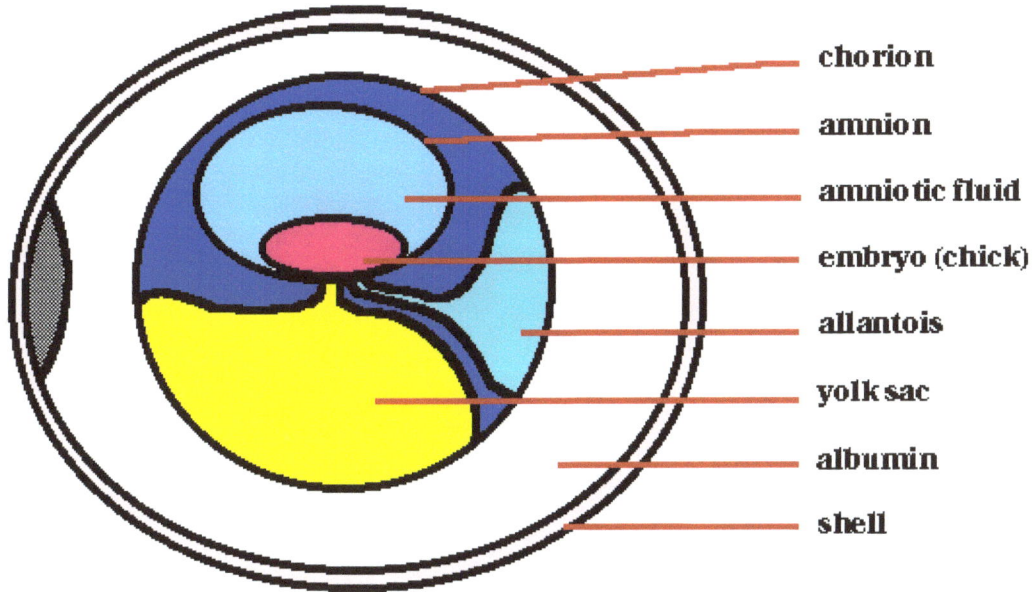

chorion

amnion

amniotic fluid

embryo (chick)

allantois

yolk sac

albumin

shell

Structure	Function
amnion	provides a watery environment for the embryo
yolk sac	contains the food for the embryo
allantois	stores waste
chorion	allows oxygen to enter and carbon dioxide to leave
albumin	egg white; protects yolk and provides additional nutrition

Some terms you may need to know:

Oviparous - eggs are laid and incubated outside the body

Ovoviviparous - eggs are incubated inside the body, born live

Viviparous - live birth, no egg (human)

Credit: biologycorner.com

33

Lace monitor laying eggs in a termite mound. Credit: bbc.co.uk

In many Asian countries, lizard eggs are a food delicacy.

Credit: dessertcomesfirst.com

Local man with a Bengal monitor *(V. Bengalensis).*   Credit: Yogesh Khandke (Wikimedia Commons)

India.   Credit: maps-asia.blogspot.com

Bengal monitors – no, not dancing. Fighting!   Credit: carnivoraforum.com

6 FIERCE FIGHTS AND BAD TEMPERS

Monitors are not social creatures. Although a male monitor will mate with a female in his territory, they rarely cooperate in food gathering or in other daily life activities. (Some Nile monitors have been observed to work in pairs to steal crocodile eggs, however!) Monitors may share carrion among themselves, but they have also been known to fight over food, territory, and mates. They do not raise their young, either together or apart. Eggs are laid, and hatchlings must fend for themselves.

Fighting among monitors

With their sharp teeth and claws, monitors are well-equipped to do battle with other animals or with each other. Dr. Neugebauer described what happens when monitors fight each other:

In male rivalry fights, the combatants are more restrained and generally do not use their teeth, claws, or tail. Each male stands up on its hind legs, and they face each other. Each attempts to push its opponent over, either to the side or backward. The goal here is to subdue the opponent and not to kill him. …Competition over food is another matter, and fights here can result in bloody injuries.

Two Komodo dragons fighting over a mate   Credit: itsnature.org

Researchers have learned, through observation, that before Komodo dragons begin their fight both participants vomit and empty their bowels to clear their digestive tracts before the battle. This, coupled with the already unpleasant odor the lizards emit due to eating carrion and producing over fifty strains of bacteria in their saliva, makes a dragon lizard fight something of an olfactory nightmare for onlookers.

For the most part, monitors are attempting to knock their opponents down and then look for some sign of submission to indicate that the fight is over and there is a clear winner. Monitors do get injured in fights, however. Dr. Auffenberg and other researchers documented the scars, scratches, and missing or damaged tails and other body parts on each of the animals they studied. Although rules of behavior in the wild are not written down (and the animals could not read them even if they were!), most animals "read" one another's body language very well and try to avoid fights whenever possible. Nevertheless, shortages of food, encroachment on one another's territory, and competition for mating rights can lead to some dangerous encounters.

Two dragon males fighting over a mate.   Credit: AFP/Komodo National Park/File

Komodo dragons fighting.   Credit: fmariani22, sportdiver.com

"Ora gila"

Although most monitors do not attack humans unless cornered or provoked, there are exceptions to this rule, too. The dragon described in the opening chapter of this book was well-known to Dr.Auffenberg. That particular dragon was thought to have been responsible for the death of one man whose body was found in the center of the lizard's home range. The lizard was called "ora gila" – the crazy Komodo monitor – by the native people. "I don't know if we can say he was crazy," said Dr. Auffenberg, "but he certainly was not normal. Perhaps he had been out in the sun too long. In any case, he was a lizard to be respected."

Dr. Auffenberg's research group learned of several attacks and at least one killing of natives by Komodo dragons. But much more common were lizard attacks on other animals. Livestock, such as goats and chickens, pet dogs and cats, wild deer and boars, and local small prey such as snakes, rabbits, rodents, and birds most often made up the monitors' meals. When a Komodo dragon kills a large animal, such as a water buffalo, he may not need to eat again for a month! So perhaps a full lizard is a safe lizard. Nevertheless, native people guarded their children lest they become the next Komodo dragon meal. And they often offered the dragons a goat or two to keep them satisfied.

Intelligence

Lizards are intelligent and curious animals, despite what people say about a "reptilian brain." The reptilian brain (or reptilian complex) is supposed to be responsible for instinctual behaviors that are involved in aggression, dominance, territoriality, and ritual displays. But animal researchers have noted that play behavior (a feature usually associated with animal species exhibiting higher cognitive abilities) exists among the large lizard species as well. And some monitors seem to be able to count up to six piece of food.

According to Gordon Burghardt, a scientist who studied Kraken, a Komodo dragon lizard bred and raised in captivity at the National Zoo, researchers observed that she could discriminate between prey and non-prey, had different playful responses to various objects presented to her, and was quite curious and investigative. She seemed to enjoy playing with a Frisbee and would sometimes pull objects out of people's pockets. She was even videotaped played tug-of-war with her keeper, just for the fun of it. Other monitor species have been observed to exhibit similar behaviors.

These observations suggest that large reptiles may be capable of higher cognition and more complex thought than was previously believed, although play behavior *was* reported in Komodo dragons as early as 1928. Even turtles appear to enjoy play!

Watch how Kraken played with her keeper on youtube.com:
http://www.youtube.com/watch?v=lp0apO2QSpc

Not man's best friend

Although only the Komodo dragons have attacked and killed humans, the personalities of other monitors are not much sweeter. Herpetologists find that most monitor lizards are aggressive, hyperactive, and unpredictable. Many researchers have teeth marks on their fingers or legs to prove it!

Monitors are evidently not afraid of the scent of human beings. When natives or visiting scientists leave their quarters, they often return to find that their supplies have been ransacked. Of course, as has been noted, domestic animals on farms are not safe, either.

Some monitors have been tamed, however. In zoos, they quickly learn to recognize their keepers, answer to their names, and find their way around their new environments. Even in the wild, some researchers have made "pets" of monitors they were studying. One lizard was often known to go swimming with its human "friend." But monitors remain wild animals, and any friendships they make take a back seat to their empty stomachs. As Keith Stewart learned when his "friend" Cedric bit him on the thumb, man's best friend is probably still his dog.

Zoo Celebrates Virgin Birth of Komodo Dragons

Wed., Jan. 25, 2007   A/P Associated Press

Flora, the Komodo dragon who resides at Chester Zoo

CHESTER, England — Scientists unveiled five squirmy black and yellow Komodo dragons Wednesday that were the product of a virgin birth, predicting that the hatchlings offered hope for breeding the endangered species.

Flora, the Komodo dragon, has produced five hatchlings although a male has never been close to her, the proud staff at the Chester Zoo said.

"Flora is oblivious to the excitement she has caused, but we are delighted to say she is now a mum and dad," said a delighted Kevin Buley, the zoo's curator of lower vertebrates and invertebrates.

The shells began cracking last week, after an eight-month gestation period, which culminated with arrival on Tuesday of the fifth dragon. Two more eggs remained to be hatched.

"The implications for conservation breeding programs are enormous because this opens up a new way that animals can potentially colonize an island," Buley said. "A female could swim to a new island, lay a clutch of eggs, then mate with sons and be sexually producing normally within a generation."

The dragons range from 16 inches to nearly 18 inches long (40 to 45 centimeters) and weigh between 3½ and 4½ ounces (100 to 125 grams), Buley said.

Eating crickets and locusts

The hatchlings were in good health and feeding on a diet of crickets and locusts.

When fully grown to 10 feet (3 meters) long and weighing about 300 pounds (135 kilograms), they'll be capable of eating a whole pig or deer at one sitting, hooves and all.

That ravenous appetite explains why Flora isn't allowed anywhere near her offspring.

"No maternal instincts exist in Komodos so it is perfectly natural to keep them as far apart as possible," Buley said. "She would try to eat anything that comes in front of her."

About 70 reptile species including snakes and lizards are known to reproduce asexually in a process known as parthenogenesis. But Flora's virginal conception, and that of another Komodo dragon in April at the London Zoo, are the first documented in Komodo dragons.

The two virgin conceptions were announced in September in a scientific paper in the journal Nature.

Endangered lizards

Komodos are native to the arid volcanic Lesser Sunda Islands in Indonesia, and are named for the island where they were discovered in 1910.

The giant lizards are considered endangered, with fewer than 4,000 surviving in the wild and facing encroachment from humans.

Komodo dragon hatchling.   Credit: corsiphoto, photobucket.com

From http://news.bbc.co.uk, Wednesday, 20 December 2006:

'Virgin births' for giant lizards

Another captive-bred female called Sungai, at London Zoo in the UK, produced four offspring earlier this year - more than two years after her last contact with a male, the scientists reported in a recent paper.

Again, genetic tests revealed the Komodo dragon babies, which are healthy and growing normally, were produced through parthenogenesis. Sungai was also able to reproduce sexually, producing another baby offspring after mating with a male called Raja. Richard Gibson, an author on the paper and a curator at the Zoological Society of London, said: "Parthenogenesis has been described before in about 70 species of vertebrates, but it has always been regarded to be a very unusual, perhaps abnormal phenomenon."

It has been shown in some snakes, fish, a monitor lizard, and even a turke, he said. "But we have seen this in two separate, unrelated female Komodo dragons within a year, so this suggests maybe parthenogenesis is much more widespread and common than previously considered." He added, "Because these animals were in captivity for years without male access, they reproduced parthenogenetically. But the ability to reproduce parthenogenetically is obviously an ancestral capability."

He said the lizards could make use of the ability to reproduce asexually when, for example, a lone female was washed up alone on an island with no males to breed with. Because of the genetics of this process, he added, her children would always be male. This is because Komodo dragons have W and Z chromosomes - females have one W and one Z, males have two Zs.

The egg from the female carries one chromosome, either a W or Z, and when parthenogenesis takes place, either the W or Z is duplicated. This leads to eggs which are WW and ZZ. WW eggs are not viable, but ZZ eggs are, and lead to male baby Komodo dragons.

And like Sungai, she would be able to switch back to sexual reproduction, so she could breed to establish a new colony. The researchers said that, to ensure genetic diversity of Komodo dragons kept in captivity, zoos should perhaps keep males and females together to avoid asexual reproduction.

There are fewer than 4,000 Komodo dragons in the wild, and they are found in three islands in Indonesia: Komodo, Flores and Rinca.

One of Sungai's offspring.

7 GIANT LIZARDS AND MAN

The monitor has been linked to stories and beliefs that simply aren't true. For example, Egyptian folklore says that the monitor sucks milk from sheep and goats and is therefore bad luck for the shepherd. Some Malaysians believe that when crocodile eggs hatch, the female tries to eat all the young that run away from the water. The hatchlings that escape to the shore become monitor lizards. Still other people believe that if a monitor lizard is watching you and sees your teeth, you will be the victim of some terrible misfortune.

The only serious predator that the giant lizards need to fear is man. Asian monitors have been used as food by man for centuries. They are killed for their meat and are used in soups and teas. Some superstitions make the monitors' body fat valuable in medicines. The fat is said to cure skin infections, arthritis, rheumatism, and even poor eyesight. Young monitors are used in a mixture of herbs, spices, and alcohol and sold as a **tonic** (health drink) for the young and the very old to drink.

In Asia, the fashion industry uses lizard hides to make purses, belts, wallets, and shoes, much like alligator skins are used. Some tribal groups still use monitor lizard skins to make ceremonial drums and other musical instruments. Stuffed monitors with eyes made out of marbles are sold by the thousands as souvenirs.

The Komodo dragon is losing its chief natural prey – hog deer and wild boar – to local hunters. Soon, there may not be enough wildlife on the dragons' islands to sustain their population.

All monitor lizards are considered **endangered** (vulnerable to extinction), but the giant lizards in particular need protection. These sometimes beautiful, often mysterious creatures may disappear if not fully protected. Breeding monitors in captivity is a tricky business. The giant lizards require large territories, specific diets, and controlled temperatures to breed successfully. Even zoos with experienced herpetology experts have not always had good luck breeding monitors. If the giant lizards become extinct – as well they might – the world will have lost a most fascinating group of reptiles.

Hunting for monitors.   Credit: e-msjed.com

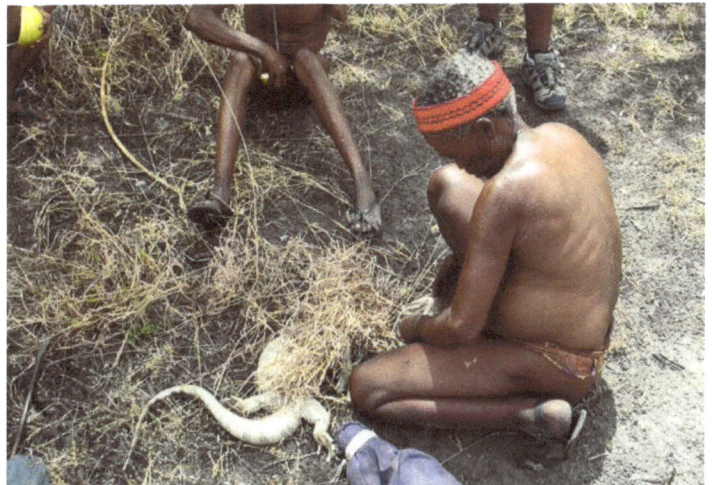

Namibian Bushman wrapping a fresh kill.   Credit: robt@jelldragon.com

★from the news★

FROM: http://www.telegraphindia.com | Calcutta, India | Thursday, August 26, 2010

A poacher carrying a number of dead monitor lizards in Kendrapara. (Telegraphindia picture)

Note to monitor lizard poachers:
Aquatic animal on verge of extinction as primitive tribe goes for the kill
By OUR CORRESPONDENT

Paradip, Aug. 25: The monitor lizards *(varanus bengalensis),*which were once found abundant in water bodies and nullahs, are on the verge of extinction, thanks to the practice of unabated poaching and laxity in vigil on part of the forest officials.

These aquatic animals play the scavenging agents in keeping the water bodies free from harmful insects and bugs.

"These aquatic animals are being killed indiscriminately. It is the people belonging to the primitive Kela tribe who are resorting to poach these animals in various places across Jagatsinghpur and Kendrapara district. The Kela settlers consume its meat while its skin and hides fetch them good money," said secretary of wildlife society Biswajit Mohanty.

"The tribes are little aware of the fact that poaching monitor lizards is an offence. As a result, the number of this aquatic species is rapidly on the downslide," he said.

The skin and hides of these aquatic animals are used for making the musical instruments.

"The Indian monitor lizard is treated as an endangered species and it is accorded protection under the Wildlife Protection Act, 1972. Because of their endangered status, these aquatic animals have also been listed under the Red Data Book to Appendix I of the CITES (Convention for International Trade in Endangered Species of Flora and Fauna)," Mohanty said.

Though poaching the monitor lizards is on the increase, yet not a single wildlife offence connected to it has been registered for almost a decade.

Thousands of musical instruments, made of the skins of monitor lizard, are sold at the Joranda fair every year.

"We have seized the products and stopped the sale of such instruments at the Joranda fair. However, there are other fairs that lend credence to the fact that poaching of lizards is still a money-making practice," Mohanty said.

The state has a dubious track record in flourishing trade in the wildlife products like ivory, skins, fresh water turtles, live birds, live snakes, snake skins and crocodile skins.

However, it is a cognisable offence. Offenders found killing, trapping or selling such products are punishable up to seven years in jail.

The wildlife wing is quite aware of such malpractice. However, with lack of vigil and enforcement, the trade is carried out openly.

The wildlife wing hardly carries out raids to curb lizard poaching. A raid on Kela villages and settlements would lead to the seizure of the skins which are usually stretched out in the open to get them dried up.

"We are yet to receive reports about the commercial trade of monitor lizards. However, the forest department would conduct raids to curb such illegal practices," said Kujang forest range officer.

Once found abundantly along water bodies and nullah, there has been a steady decline in number of monitor lizard, a delicate aquatic species that figures in the list of endangered species.

Unabated poaching and absence of forest officials' vigil have contributed to gross decimation of these aquatic animals that are used to play scavenging agents in keeping the water bodies free from harmful insects and bugs.

The skin and hides form an important component in the making of musical instruments. The lizards' hide figure prominently on the indigenous musical instruments otherwise called 'khanjani' in local parlance. "Khanjani" is made of a small hollow round ring of wood on which a tanned monitor lizard skin is stretched round.

From Wikipedia.org: Wildlife Trade

The international **wildlife trade** is a serious conservation problem, addressed by the United Nations' Convention of International Trade in Endangered Species of Wild Fauna and Flora CITES, which currently has 175 member countries called Parties. The 15th meeting of the Parties took place in Doha, Qatar during 13–25 March 2010. Wildlife trade consists of the trade, barter, or sale of wild specimens of animals and plants. It impacts many thousands of species which may be traded live, whole, or as a wide variety of parts, pieces and derivatives. The great diversity of items and products traded can make it very difficult to identify the species being traded. Species identification poses a significant challenge to authorities when responding to international wildlife trade....

In August 2010, a notorious Malaysian wildlife trader has been arrested after having tried to smuggle about 100 live snakes to Indonesia. Since the early 1980s, he legally wholesaled tens of thousands of wild reptiles annually, many of which were on sale in American pet stores. But he allegedly commanded one of the world's largest **wildlife trafficking** syndicates, and using a private zoo as a cover, also offered a large array of contraband, including snow leopard pelts, panda bear skins, rhino horns, rare birds, and Komodo dragons, chinchillas, elephants, gorillas, tigers, and smuggled critically endangered wildlife from Australia, China, Madagascar, New Zealand, South America to markets largely in Europe, Japan, and the United States.

★ biography ★

CLAUDIO CIOFI, CONSERVATION BIOLOGIST

Credit: yale.edu

Dr. Claudio Ciofi is one of the world's leading authorities on the Komodo dragon lizard. He was born in Italy, but speaks four languages, including English. He studied at the University of Kent at Canterbury in England and at the Yale University Department of Evolutionary Ecology and Biology.

Today, Dr. Ciofi manages the Komodo dragon population on four island at Komodo National Park. One of his chief goals is to persuade the indigenous community that the Komodo dragon is not merely a pest who threatens their livestock, but a valuable asset to their lives. He hopes to encourage the villagers to accept the dragons as a part of their heritage and history and help them harness the dragons' appeal to visiting tourists. In this way, Dr. Ciofi plans to make conserving the Komodo dragon lizard congruent with improving the villagers' lives. Once the native population sees the Komodo dragon as a positive factor in their economy and livelihood, Dr. Ciofi believes conservation efforts will meet with greater cooperation.

Many obstacles are yet to be overcome. Habitat encroachment and competition by humans for the dragons' main prey – deer and pig – are serious issues that need resolution. But Dr. Ciofi is convinced that once the villagers – not just scientists and conservationists – take ownership of the problems and the solutions, the outcome will be extremely positive for the dragons as well as the villagers.

The dragons have evidently already disappeared from the largest island they previously inhabited, Flores. Dr. Ciofi and his colleagues are committed to resolving the issues so that man and nature can once again live in harmony. For the Komodo dragons, this is a matter of life or death.

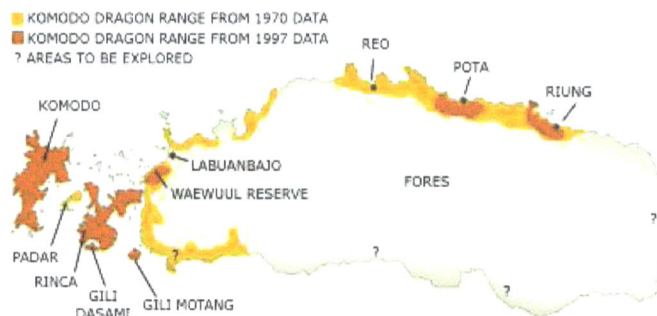

KOMODO DRAGON RANGE FROM 1970 DATA
KOMODO DRAGON RANGE FROM 1997 DATA
? AREAS TO BE EXPLORED

REO
POTA
RIUNG
KOMODO
LABUANBAJO
WAEWUUL RESERVE
FORES
PADAR
RINCA
GILI DASAMI
GILI MOTANG

Credit: Scientific American

46

Conservation efforts

Conservation is the careful utilization and protection of a natural resource in order to prevent its depletion, injury, waste, or loss. Conservation is preservation.

Many monitor species, as well as other animal species, are captured and sold by local people for financial reasons, and this can lead to their depletion or even their extinction. Often, in places like New Guinea, the Philippines, Ghana, Indonesia, and elsewhere, poverty is the driving force behind the capture and sale of animals. People in such circumstances can do serious damage to the monitor population because they are not aware of the consequences of their actions. Education is seen as the solution.

Dr. Daniel Bennett, of the Department of Zoology at the University of Aberdeen, Scotland, works with the Mampam Conservation organization to help endangered and neglected people, wildlife and habitats find practical solutions to serious problems that impact society, ecology, and biodiversity. He describes a typical scenario in the monitor lizard trade:

Adult female monitor lizards are extremely difficult to find outside the breeding season (typically we catch 6 - 10 adult males for every female we encounter). They appear to limit their movements to searching for food and accumulating energy to produce eggs. During the breeding season the females become extremely active as they search for good nesting sites. At this time of year they are easy to collect. The animals are kept in captivity, often in very unsanitary conditions, until they produce eggs which are then incubated artificially. As soon as they hatch they can be exported as extremely cute babies, not taken from the wild but "captive hatched" from mothers "released into the wild." In fact these [female] animals, now exhausted and stressed, are almost guaranteed to perish. There is little incentive for the "farmer" to actually return them. It would be impractical to take each one back to the place it was caught, and more often than not the lizards are either recycled into the pet trade, sold for meat and skin, or just dumped at a roadside. In a few cases (such as in Ghana) government departments collect the animals from different exporters and release thousands of them at a time. There is no evidence that any of these animal have ever survived to breed the following year. In countries such as Indonesia, where the females have been brought by boat from some distant island, death is inevitable.

Only the most cynical and desperate of poachers catch pregnant animals. In most hunting societies they are the only animals afforded protection, because without them the population will decline. However, the pet trade saw in gravid [pregnant] monitor lizards the opportunity to greatly reduce their overheads and fool their customers into thinking that their animals were collected "with conservation in mind."

(www.mampam.com)

Who exactly are the purchasers of these abducted animals? Almost all of the animals are sold to the pet trade in North America, Europe, and Japan, although some are sold as exotic foods. These are highly industrialized countries where the standard of living is usually much higher than that of the countries where the animals are captured. Often the end-purchasers of these lizards have been led to believe that they were "farm raised" or "ranched," but the facts show otherwise.

Dr. Bennett says the **exporters** may or may not understand the consequences of what they are doing. But the **importers** most certainly do. "But although animal exporters around the world have always been happy to help us, no animal *importers* in North America, Europe or Japan have ever offered to cooperate." Evidently, the lure of financial gain often makes people commit atrocities against nature.

Many conservation organizations work to right these wrongs. Often they rely on volunteers or graduate students to do much of the work that must be done. But they also need financial support to continue their work. People interested in seeing giant lizards (and other animal groups) survive should consider donating to a conservation organization of their choice. These organizations often make a substantial difference in the lives of both people and animals in emerging and underdeveloped countries.

★from the news★

New Giant Lizard Discovered in the Philippines!

By Susan Milius, *Science News* | April 7, 2010

Scientists couldn't see the lizard for the trees. But now they've tracked down and named *Varanus bitatawa*, a skittish reptile that's hard to spot even though it grows up to 2 meters long and sports bright yellow speckles.

In forests on the Philippine island of Luzon, the newly discovered monitor lizard hauls itself up into trees in search of fruit and melts into the vegetation if humans approach, says herpetologist Rafe Brown of the Biodiversity Institute at the University of Kansas in Lawrence. He and his colleagues described and named the species in a paper published online the week of April 5 in *Biology Letters*.

The species is "new to us," Brown clarifies, because the Agta and Ilongot peoples living in forests of the Sierra Madre range know the lizard well — as a delicacy. It mostly eats fruit and reportedly tastes better than a much more common scavenging monitor that's "attracted to stinky stuff," Brown says.

A cousin to the giant Komodo dragon, *Varanus bitatawa* is hard to find but once detected, is pretty hard to ignore. During adulthood, yellow markings differentiate it from a much drabber neighbor — though both species sport colorful patterns as juveniles.

Reptile systematist Michael B. Harvey, who was not part of Brown's group, has helped name another *Varanus* lizard from New Guinea and examined specimens from Southeast Asia. "I quickly realized that the diversity of these lizards had been greatly underestimated," says Harvey, of Broward College in Davie, Florida. "I only hope that we don't lose much of this biodiversity before scientists can study it."

Deforestation poses a major threat to the biodiversity of the Philippines, which Brown and his colleagues describe in their paper as a "global conservation hot spot."

Western scientists first glimpsed the big monitor in 2001, Brown says, when biologists exploring the forest happened on hunters carrying a large lizard home for dinner. The biologists were permitted to photograph it, but theirs was the first of several encounters in which hunters showed no interest in giving up the centerpiece of a big family meal.

Herpetologist Arvin Diesmos of the National Museum of the Philippines in Manila and other researchers persisted in collecting photographs, local intelligence and the occasional juvenile, but they could not secure a full-grown adult specimen.

Then, in the summer of 2009, a team led by Brown and his graduate student Luke Welton got its hands on an adult lizard. They documented identifying anatomical characteristics such as the distinctive little horns on the ends of the lizards' double-barreled male reproductive organs. Which, by the way, are far from unusual in and of themselves: "All snakes and lizards have a paired copulatory organ," Brown says.

DNA tests were even more important, confirming that the species differs from a previously identified fruit-eating monitor living in a different part of the island.

Brown actually learned of the adult specimen's existence via text message. After he and his students spent weeks in the mountains surveying other vertebrates and hoping for an adult *Varanus bitatawa*, Brown had to return home early to start the fall semester. But he received a message from his students in the expedition's final hours announcing their success — and letting him know that they were having a hard time finding a way to get from their camp to the airport!

For More Information

Auffenberg, Walter (1981). *The Behavioral Ecology of the Komodo Monitor*. Gainesville: University Press of Florida. ISBN 978-0813006215.

Auffenberg, Walter (1994). *The Bengal Monitor*. Gainesville: University Press of Florida. ISBN 0813012953.

Bennett, Daniel (1995). *A Little Book of Monitor Lizards*. Glossop, UK: Viper Press. ISBN 978-0952663218.

Burghardt, Gordon M.; Sutton-Smith, Brian (2006). *The Genesis of Animal Play: Testing the Limits*. Cambridge, MA: MIT Press. ISBN 978-0262524698.

Ciofi, Claudio (1999). The Komodo Dragon. *Scientific American* 280 (3):84-91.

Gibbons, J. Whitfield; Odum, Eugene P. (1983). *Their Blood Runs Cold: Adventures With Reptiles and Amphibians*. Tuscaloosa: University of Alabama Press. ISBN 978-0817301354.

Isaacs, Jennifer (2006). *Australian Dreaming: 40,000 Years of Aboriginal History*. Chatswood NSW: New Holland Publishers. ISBN 978-1741102581.

King, Dennis; Green, Brian; Knight, Frank; Newgrain, Keith (1999). *Monitors: The Biology of Varanid Lizards*. Malabar, FL: Krieger Publishing Company. ISBN 978-1575241128.

Molnar, Ralph (2004). *Dragons in the Dust: The Paleobiology of the Giant Monitor Lizard Megalania*. Bloomington: Indiana University Press. ISBN 978-0253343741.

Murphy, James B. (2002). *Komodo Dragons: Biology and Conservation*. Wash., DC: Smithsonian Books. ISBN 978-1588340733.

Murphy, James B; Walsh, Trooper (2006). Dragons and humans. *Herpetological Review* 37(3):269-275.

NATURE (2009). *The Dragon Chronicles (DVD)*. Questar. (With Rom Whitaker)

NOVA (2010). *Lizard Kings (DVD)*. PBS. (With Erick Pianka)

Pianka, Erick; King, Dennis (Editors) (2004). *Varanoid Lizards of the World*, Bloomington: Indiana University Press. ISBN 978-0253343666.

Stewart, Keith (1982). Cedric of Umbrawarra. *Audubon* 84(1): 96-101.

www.ingramcontent.com/pod-product-compliance
Lightning Source LLC
Chambersburg PA
CBHW060847270326
41934CB00002B/33